The Prepper's Guide To Off The Grid Survival

An Introduction Into Living A Self Sufficient, Stress Free Lifestyle In Financial Peace

By Henry Hill

Disclaimer

This book is intended to be a general guide, to raise
awareness, and to help people make informed decisions in
the context of their own personal circumstance.

The author accepts no responsibility for any loss or injury
be it personal or financial, as a result for the use or misuse
of the information in this book. If you have any doubts or
concerns after reading this book, please speak to a qualified
person before taking any actions.

Contents

Introduction

Modernity has turned life into an inter-connected network or web of *things*. And, I am not using "network" as a keyword for social media or the "web" for the internet. What I am discussing predates social media and the internet by far.

Connected refers to your life and wallet. You work to earn money just to have a thousand demands on that money. Let's think about the American Dream: buying a house in suburbia, with a white picket fence to boot. That partial picture of life seems to be just that, a dream.

You have this house and with it you get it all. You get water from the tap, electricity from the wall, toilet water that just magically disappears into the sewage system. But there is more to it still.

That image being put in your head does not mention the monthly electric bill that accompanies it. Or the water bill? What about the cost of sewage? Telephone connection? The idea of being a homeowner sounds so great because most times, it is not a full picture of the burden it requires. You don't realize the weight put on your shoulders when you are doing it. It is like tricking the Titan Atlas all over again.

No matter what your feelings are on the Amish, they got something right. They aren't part of the "grid" of things. They don't worry about these bills and their life goes on. Sure, they don't have a television set to watch these imposter shows about their culture but they don't have the pressure of paying for it either. Hell, they put back their towns quicker after hurricane-level winds came through than New York City, the spitting image of being connected and modern, did.

Maybe you are reading this because you are in this position. Maybe you are not even a homeowner yet and are just reading this on a whim or because you are curious. Regardless of your reason for flipping through the pages of my book, I hope this enlightens you to how things really are in the typical life on the grid, and what things could be like off the grid.

The Purpose of this Book

I am putting this book together to be not only a survival guide but a beacon of hope. I want to show people this is possible. I want to show people that life off the grid isn't for outcasts or childhood fantasies.

Like most people growing up, you probably read the novel *My Side of the Mountain*. For those that haven't, a young boy leaves home and sets out for life in the wilderness of the mountains. He finds shelter, hunts and gathers, and ultimately has a peaceful existence away from it all. In fact, the boy's family eventually decides to join him.

For most of you that sounds too good to be true but it isn't. It is true. That boy is happy because of the simplicity and not having the pressures of the typical connected life.

The fact that people see the American Dream as something to strive for, versus the independence and the freedom of living off the grid, is bewildering to me. It is possible to live a full life and to be a productive part of society without being dependent on it.

Chapter 1

Living on the Grid vs Living off the Grid

The principle differences between on the grid and off the grid are pressures and dependence. But I am not here to fool you. I'm not a shoddy salesman. I want to inform you. To the best of my ability I would like you to have the information at your fingertips that compare these two lifestyles. Ahead of time, I would like to apologize for if I do come off biased towards one of these lifestyle choices but it is what I am now.

Living on the Grid

Life on the grid can seem just great sometimes. For those top-ten percenters it probably seems just great, all of the time but even that I doubt. The rest go to work, most probably do their nine-to-five and you go home.
Parts of life become mechanical and thoughtless. You perform tasks and you earn money. You get so busy you go out to eat as much as you can, money goes out. Utilities come in your house, money goes out. You wait for those newest consumer purchases that sprout up every year around Christmas, money goes out.
Essentially, this is the classic case of economies of scale. You are so good at your job, you can perform it more efficiently than others while others are more efficient at building products, cooking food, or providing utilities so they come to you. In a way it is a trade off on time but it is a loss of quality and a loss of meaning.
What does that meal mean to you?
What does your purchase mean to you today? What about next year?

And then what happens when the power goes out? You have to wait for someone to get to it. It could be a few hours. What about if an entire town loses electricity? You could be on hold until all the other repairs are made before you get your service. This is what I mean by the Amish handling things off the grid. They rebuilt entire towns, out of their own sweat and labor rather than waiting for others. They got their lives back to normal before the Big Apple got their lights back on.

To continue, what happens when you are not satisfied with something? Your purchase breaks or the service somewhere is awful. Do you get on the phone and try to talk to their customer service? Not if you want to maintain your head of hair.

This is the mechanical part. Everything seems detached and repetitive.

Living off the Grid

Living off the grid on the other hand is not so much about being disconnected but about doing things yourself; it's about taking responsibility for yourself and not in a monotonous or burdening way. If something is not working, it is because of you. That is not so gloomy because guess who can fix it? You can!

You don't necessarily have to live without electricity. You can if you want but that is your choice. If you still want electricity, you can produce it yourself. You don't have to negate hundreds of years of human advancement to live off the grid. Instead, you can produce it remotely without being connected to, quite literally, the power grid.

Running water is more obvious because people pumping in their own well water is a lot more prominent. Considering that the US government puts fluoride in municipal water systems, it goes without saying a lot of people are against this forced alteration of water. It is surprising how many fresh water sources there are around you, but we'll look at that later.

At this point, you just have to understand that all things can be done on your own, without being dependent on utilities for everything or the tax that comes on top of that. You don't have to be dependent on others either. If a problem surfaces, you are the solution to that.

Your frustration goes down a lot when you realize that you are the problem to things because you can fix you but you can't fix other people's problems.

Moving on from utilities though, you can do almost everything on your own. Growing your own fruit and vegetables is manageable in a decent sized personal garden. Additionally, raising a small amount of livestock is more manageable than you'd assume. Plus, you don't have to worry about chemicals used in industrial farming or the way food is handled during processing.

At this point you are basically producing off the land. Utilities come from the area, crops and animals grow from the land, and your shelter is built right into it. But you can still go further. You can begin to craft your own skills of … just that, crafting. Building and making things on your own.

If you are thinking at this point, "He's just telling me you can do this without really giving me information." I applaud your attentiveness. I will be showing you how this is possible in the coming chapters. I just want to open your eyes now.

Chapter 2

Living without Public Utilities

In the previous chapter, it was mentioned several times that it is possible to live without paying for these public utilities that you have to pay for monthly. Let's look at each utility in turn and discuss viable alternatives to each.

Alternatives to Public Electricity

Electricity is an easy alternative to consider because it has been in the public spotlight quite frequently. With a down economy and people being more conscience about environmental degradation, it is natural that there would be concerns with public electricity, whether it is coal, gas, nuclear, or whatever else you may be getting. The best alternative for you really is based on what you have at your disposal. Do you have constant sunlight or wind? Do you have a powerful enough stream running by your property? What would you even need electricity for?

Solar Power, Hydro Electrical and Wind Power are the main sources of power available to you when living off the grid

Currently, one of the most prominent alternatives to public electricity is solar power. Solar panels are quite capable of being scaled to household use, combined with the ability to convert enough sunlight into electricity to power your needs and efficient enough batteries to save it, it offers an efficient means of electricity. Additionally, with the recent fame of private solar panels, there are even quite a few kits and guides for building these yourself.

Certainly, a windmill would offer a household a means to electricity in areas that has wind in the plenty. This goes with playing your locality to your advantage. If you have wind, use it. Windmills are available for individual household use as well.

Now another, very important, thing to consider is what do you need electricity for? We'll provide options for cooking, heating, and water later that will give you ways around electricity so you don't necessarily need it for that. If you are attached to the bright lighting only modern day light bulbs provide then by all means, continue with one of the above. But if you don't want to, candles or oil lamps are certainly an off the grid option. They are functional in the sense they give off light and can be created on your own, with materials that are readily available. We'll look at this more later.

These are all possible alternatives to public electricity. Living off the grid doesn't really discriminate between any of these aforementioned methods and you can just as easily choose any one of them you are comfortable with.

Alternatives to Public Water

For most people, public water is pumped out of a reservoir then processed by the local water authority then pumped to your house. This usually includes outdated piping, fluoride additives, and whatever the flavor of the day may be.

Now water is an absolute necessity though so we can't, as in the end of the electricity section, decide to live without it. Luckily, there are simple alternatives that most environments offer. The two easiest to consider would be to use well water or collect rain water, again you have to play your strengths.

A water well or bore may be one of the most viable ways to have a constant water supply

There are actually plenty of people living on the grid that still decide to use their own well water. This can be done in several ways but the most efficient would be pumping. You can either use a manual pump and store your water or (if you've decided to use an electricity alternative) use an electric pump that could effectively circulate water throughout your existing household plumbing. The latter option really requires very little changes to your current lifestyle but disconnects you from the grid.

Collecting rain water is typically, a very sensible thing to do and some even argue the purity of rain water far exceeds that of any other water source, as long as there is not too much air pollution in your area. You can do this as simply as using a filtered rain barrel or a more intricate

Rain water barrels are one of the easiest and most affordable ways to recycle and store pure rain water

full rainwater collecting system and cistern. Rain barrels are obviously cheaper and easier to put together however a full system is more efficient and will provide you with more water.

A full system can provide enough water for everyday use and if you choose to use an electric pump you can still go on using your water system already in your house. Rain barrels don't really give this option but you can discriminate based on usage and keep some for drinking and some for watering plants or other alternative uses of water. Again, your level of involvement is purely up to you. To do so on your own, filtering systems are quite easy. A proper water filter only requires charcoal or rocks and sand. You could probably inventory most of these by just doing a quick walk around your yard.

Even rain barrels can be simpler than you are probably imagining. You don't have to think in terms of actual barrels, although you could. A barrel just has to be something with the large amount of surface space facing the sky and a funnel or spigot towards the bottom but be sure to leave room for the filter.

Alternatives to Public Sewage

Of all the off the grid solutions, this may seem the most difficult and expensive. The reason being is what is being dealt with and that is essentially waste. That ranges from everything from water used to clean to bodily waste and you probably don't want to be spending too much time with the latter of those.

A septic tank is the most obvious and viable alternative to public sewage BUT make sure to install it a good distance from your water supply.

Now, what a sewage system essentially does is two things: removes waste water from sink drains and removes waste water from toilets. An efficient system can actually reuse waste water in sinks into the toilets. Toilet water, obviously, cannot really be reused.

9

The most obvious alternative to public sewage is then a septic tank which basically takes your sewage and puts it in your own tank outside. You have to be very careful with this, especially if you are collecting your own water from a well. You want to make sure that the post-septic tank sewage distribution is far enough away from your fresh water supply that it runs clear of it or that you use a system that processes it enough to not contaminate it.

Alternatives to Household Heat

Again, this is another topic of interest recently for people seeking to lower costs and if you live in a heavily wooded area it is easy! Another locational concern would be based on how severe your winters are. Your options here are good, old fashioned fireplaces, internal wood burners or larger, remote wood burners.

A fireplace is nice and very simple household heating utility if you don't have a very

Vintage wood stoves like this were designed when there was no grid so they can not only heat your home and cook your food but some of them also feature wet backs which can provide you with a constant supply of hot water

large area or if you experience milder cool periods. The problem with fireplaces is their efficiency and confinement to basically a single room (unless you have many fireplaces). But, at least they make for a relaxing environment.

Compared to fireplaces, wood burners are a lot more efficient and can easily be connected to an entire house the same way a furnace does. Now just to explain efficiency here, burning less wood equals more heat which is great if you are gathering wood on your own and for cold winters, especially prolonged ones. If your needs require heating an entire house, an internal wood burner unit would be enough for you.

An external unit would only be necessary if you have a very large and open home. And, you only need to multiply all things from the internal wood burner. If your external is twice as large, you need to do twice as much work but it will heat twice as much. Get it?

There is word of warning for using wood to heat your house though. You must be forward thinking and plan ahead.

The best wood to burn is wood that is seasoned. You want to burn old wood, not wood you cut yesterday and generally not even this year.

Alternatives for Cooking Fuels and Oils

Since we've already looked at alternatives for heat, you can bake using certain wood stoves without a problem. You can grill. You can even get fireplaces with pizza stoves. But, now we need something to burn the stovetop if you are used to a gas range to continue with a typical lifestyle. In fact, if you decide to produce electricity you can still use an electric range. Again, your choice is yours.

This section is going to look at two things because they are very closely related: make fuels to burn and making oils to lubricate your pan. Not only are they used for the same purpose, but you can also grow the required ingredients basically on your property, and we'll visit that topic more in the following chapters. First let's look at making fuels.

The easiest way to make a flammable fuel to cook with is to make ethanol. The ethanol process is relatively simple and inexpensive. To start this you will need a few things, including a container to ferment, yeast, and a still. You will also need a base for the ethanol, something that is very starchy such as corn, potatoes, or sugar. That is really the part that matters because you can grow those in most climates!

The next part is cooking oil so just look for a moment in your pantry to see what you have in there. Well, olive oil may be a bit difficult because olives may be difficult to grow unless you live in the right area. We'll look at more readily available sources for oil that have a high yield. So keep looking in that pantry.

You probably have some vegetable or sunflower oil. Because of the ease of growing sunflowers, let's look at that. There are two options with making sunflower oil, one contains no specialty equipment whereas the other requires an oil extractor. Without an oil extractor it is a much longer and time consuming process, and since it will be your main or only means for cooking oil, it is best to just foot the bill and get the oil extractor. It will be worth it in the long run. All you have to do is grow sunflowers, then dry the heads so the seeds fall off and then grind it. It is as simple as this and then you can let this settle. The oil needs a cool-down period and then you can skim the actual cooking oil off the top and use it, 5 to 10 days is enough.

Conclusion

This has been a very heavy chapter so let's recap this chapter to collect what we've looked at so far:

"Grid" Utility	Ideal Off the Grid Alternatives	Other Off the Grid Alternatives
Electricity	Household Solar/Wind Power	Candles
Water	Automated well pump or rain collecting system	Rain barrels or hand pumps
Sewage	Septic tank	Out house
Heat	Wood burner	Fireplace
Gas or Electricity for Cooking	Make ethanol from any number of plant sources	(Use your electricity)
Cooking Oil	Sunflower Oil	Other vegetables

The aim of this chapter was not to teach you how to do every single part of this, rather just open your eyes to the possibilities and to provide you with an inventory list. Consider this as a jumping off point. Once you've decided which route you'd like to go, you can then search for more information based on that.

Chapter 3

The Basics to Growing your own Produce

For growing your own food, you really have to consider your property size and climate to come out with the best options. It may be different for you if you live in a warmer and rainier climate than someone that has a shorter growing season, or someone in a drier climate. Additionally, some crops take a lot of space to grow whereas others' can be done in tighter spaces.

Collecting rainwater and allowing for very little waste will eliminate some of the problems associated with dry-spells but does come with an added workload. Depending on your family size and consumption habits the area of land required may be different. If you are a household of 2 that eats all vegetables, you could need up to 3/4 of an acre and as little as 1/4 if you eat more wheat (you can basically multiply up based on family size and it will give you a general enough idea). For our purposes though, we will plan this for a moderate sized piece of property, about one acre, and a temperate climate.

Planning and Preparations

The most important thing to consider is that in order to truly live off the grid you must yield enough to survive off of. So if your land is limited you have to piece together how to fit as much as possible that yields an optimal amount, in several varieties on your property. Easy, right?
It actually can be after a while. Once you find out what works and what doesn't, growing fruits and vegetables gets easier. That being said, if it is your first time at growing, I wouldn't suggest planning to go all-in at once. This may take some time and practice.
You need to section off your garden appropriately to begin. Designate a portion of your land for tree fruits, leafy greens, roots, herbs and spices, and berries and nuts (don't forget a place for your sunflowers). Make sure there are clear divisions between these because they may work in harmony together but other times they may be invasive towards other types of plants growing nearby. Encircle your garden to protect it as well. You don't want nearby rabbits and deer to run off with your food for the year.
Aside from planning out the layout, make sure to prepare the land. Remove rocks and unfriendly soil. Topsoil with natural fertilizers will keep the land fertile.

Plant Inventory

To begin you need to start thinking about your health, in a sense. You need to know what is necessary to survive and since this guide is on how to survive well off the grid, we need to go a bit beyond just basic survival. Let's break down by food group you need to survive from vegetables. Firstly, you need starches for energy so that is a good place to begin. The main sources of starch are corn, potatoes, and wheat, and all of these are easy enough to grow in most areas. Additionally, you won't have to worry about making excess and wasting because you are going to also use this for fuel. Also remember you need a place for those sunflowers for the oil.

Let's also consider your leafy greens because these have a high vitamin yield with less difficulty than fruits. Regular lettuce can almost automatically be discounted immediately and this is something important to understand. It isn't too difficult to grow but you don't get anything out of it. Why put a lot of energy and resources into an item that doesn't replenish you? Great question, easy answer: don't. Instead focus on items like carrots, spinach, and kale. Then you can grow other vegetables as well, such as carrots and tomatoes.

Fruits can be managed as well but these will generally take a long time to give anything back to you. An apple tree has to grow before you can start enjoying the fruit. So you should start growing this off the start, just don't expect apples right away, and same with grape vines. Berries can easily be grown though. We won't even get into citrusy fruits right now because it may not be manageable for most environments. However, you can grow small amounts of watermelons and strawberries during summer periods or indoors. The nice thing about fruits is excess once again because if you grow too much, you just make jam or fruit preserve and then you have it throughout the winter, and even longer.

Depending on the herbs you use, you can start growing these from a window ledge until they get large enough to be moved outside (if you require that many herbs in your diet). They can be placed near your onions and garlic, which are generally easy-to-grow items.

Most of these can be started from seeds however, it may be in your best interest to begin growing some of these from starters to speed up the growing time. Additionally, you have to consider preserving these for the following growing period. Some plants may be able to cut down to the root and will regrow, where others you have to save seeds to replant. Smaller items you can even relocate to your house so that you can still get small amounts of fresh fruits, vegetables and herbs throughout the winter, and have it started for the next summer.

Conclusion

You will grow and learn from your experiences planting just as your plants will. You will find a million books teaching you how to garden or live off the land and each one of them will tell you "the best way" of doing things. You will find your way differs slightly from theirs and that is alright. It is expected and encouraged even.

This is why you will get better at it as you go. You'll figure out ways to grow more efficiently. You will figure out what you can't get growing for one reason or another. And, more importantly, you will try new items or new ways and get better at what you are doing. This is the glory in taking initiative in your own survival. You get attached to your work and find pride and fulfillment in what you are doing.

Chapter 4

The Basics of Living with Small Livestock

This chapter is essentially a continuation of chapter 3 because they are interconnected in many ways but since there may be a few vegetarians or vegans in the audience, they have been split. Again, you need to assess your needs. If you don't need meats (for the vegetarians or vegans), you may skip this chapter. For those that do, consider which meats you need on a daily, weekly, and yearly basis. Unfortunately, for beef lovers, you'll have to go without if you have a small piece of land or for when you are just getting started.

Chickens and Rabbits

Chicken is a good place to start with here because of space and chicken products. Chickens need a very small plot of land to grow so even the smallest property can probably accommodate a chicken coop and land for them to roam around.
Building wooden chicken coop is as simple as making about a two square foot boxes for each chicken you have. You can add on in the future but you should have a few empty "boxes" for the babies!
Additionally, you only need a little larger area for them to roam around in. The most difficult thing will be getting started on raising chickens and not actually building their "homes". This is especially true for the new chicks because

it is important to keep them in a warm area which may require a temporary spot in the house, if necessary.

The benefits though are once you get started, it is a pretty easy process. Additionally, you get plenty of eggs from a small amount of chickens. Depending on your egg intake, 3 hens (even less if they are happy and young hens) should provide more than enough per person for eggs. Then, it goes without saying; there is the actual chicken meat. This is less easy to say how many days of meat you will get from chicken because it depends on your habits and the size of your chickens. You will figure out as you go.

Rabbits are very similar to raising chickens, just without eggs. They require about as much attention and space. Rabbit cages are similar in size to chicken coops and they are more resistant to cold, although you'll have to winterize their cage. The bonus to rabbits is their fur, which has additional uses so it won't go to waste. I think

The Californian Rabbit is a good choice if you are looking for a rabbit breed which will provide you with a good supply of meat and fur.

rabbit fur uses needs no introduction but you can come up with many additional uses along the way.

Pigs

Pigs are an animal that gets a bad image for being dirty but that is not necessarily the case. They produce a large quantity of meat with little effort. They are usually considered dirty because they are

careless, in just about everything. They care as much for

their hygiene as they do for the food you decide to give them. They'll eat just about anything you give them. Aside from meat pigs have very little purpose although one pig will be enough to supply you for a long time. Several pigs will feed several people months, with consuming daily. Also, pork is easily stored and if properly prepared can last a long time.

Goats and Sheep

Just because you won't be raising cows, doesn't mean you have to go without milk. Goats produce excellent milk which doesn't taste too different from cows. They don't require too much food either and will graze your high patches of grass, helping you maintain an aesthetically pleasing yard. You will have to keep in consideration the other vegetables they will consume. Essentially though, you will only need one female goat to get enough milk for daily consumption.

Sheep will need more land than goats but are equally self-sufficient. They just need enough grassland to graze off of and they will grow and be happy. It may go without saying that lamb meat is delicious no matter how fatty it is, the wool is plentiful, and the milk is usable. These make well-rounded, efficient animals to raise. To put the animals' wool into use may be a little difficult and time consuming but don't let that put you off of raising them. You can always use the wool as a raw material to trade.

Conclusion

For those of you going straight into raising livestock, butchering may be something you overlook but is very necessary, unless you plan to live off eggs and milk only. If you've never killed, gutted, and butchered an animal it may be best to learn from someone with experience first. Either someone you know or a professional butcher may be a good start for learning, although the professional butcher may be reluctant at first (be sure to inform them it is for personal use).

But, here is a list of animals that you could easily raise and each provides you with a different comfort and use. Some animals will provide eggs, dairy, a helping hand (or mouth) with yard work, and obviously, meat. In addition to the crops you are growing, it is all what you need to survive. Be sure to factor in your livestock when considering mouths to feed from your crops though.

Chapter 5

Money Management and Bartering

So I've listed many things here that you've probably been seeing price tags in your mind every time I mention something new. Well getting started does come with a price but over time it will start to pay you back by reducing upkeep costs and removing the pressure of bills. You can however try to keep your start-up costs down and try to roll out an "Off the Grid" lifestyle in a gradual way.

Financing the Start-Up

You have all the utility alternatives to purchase: solar grids or windmills or both, water pumps or rain collecting systems, septic system, and wood burner. If you choose to be thrifty, you can be. You don't have to begin purchasing the best and can even make your own – there are plenty of kits and do-it-yourself guides to making solar grids. So you can gradually implement these or start low and upgrade (manual pump to automatic later).

Seeds will save you money when you are growing and buying livestock when they are in abundance will do the same for your animal costs, then once you start producing, you can trade with others to fill in the gaps in your production. Chickens are probably the cheapest way to begin and easiest to produce more than you need.

You can grow and raise a small variety of plants and animals but make excess. You can trade that excess for new animals or seeds. Then you are making a larger variety of plants and animals which you can trade for that many more. You'll find it builds faster than you expected. So a word of advice, don't go out and buy everything from the start.

This is what I mean by building up gradually. The cost of everything at once is unnecessary.

Bartering

Tips for bartering are plain and simple. Think of what money actually is in your life – it is a means of saving your "productive time" for trading at a later time. Too much is attached to what money is because it is essentially only a tool for bartering. Now that you understand money, the only problem lies with others' consideration of money.

To start though, every area has farmers that are easily located that you can take this excess to and see if they are willing to trade. Craigslist has an online bartering system that you can find people willing to make deals in your area. You know people that probably wouldn't mind some eggs. Each of these sources has something you need. Get what you need from them and make fair trades. Don't try to rip people off or think that a barter is bargaining because you'll soon run out of people to barter with.

Don't even be afraid of "cashing in" for just that, cash, as a backup. Unfortunately, there is this emphasis on money as the only real liquid asset so you may need this for certain items (upgrading your household infrastructure) or in times of an emergency (a bad harvest season).

Conclusion

Money is a problem that we are trying to get away from in this "Off the Grid" lifestyle, not to add to. Don't allow money to become a problem for you. Limit your dependence on it and eventually alleviate it.

Also, keep your sights set on the horizon and don't think so much about the cost now as the lack thereof later. Once you convert your house to fully self-sufficient you won't have to worry about the monthly utility bills anymore. Once you have the produce and livestock needed to survive, you also won't need to foot the weekly grocery bill anymore.

Chapter 6

Dealing with Local Laws Off the Grid

With an "Off the Grid" lifestyle, you are taking a lot of things that used to be done by professionals and doing yourself. One benefit of this is that a lot of things produced for personal use do not require licenses, though some still will. I will give you a brief overall of what you should look into but since it changes from state to state and community to community it is best to check with your local government to find out for sure and stay up to date.

Firstly, your land has to be zoned and permitted for things like a septic system. Not every piece of land can just simply have a septic tank installed but if the case is that the tank cannot be installed, there are ways around it. Those ways just come with an additional bill. You can cross that bridge when you get there.

Next is what you are producing. If you are trying to produce ethanol for fuel, you will need to prove that: 1. It is for personal use and 2. It is for fuel and not for drinking. The government frowns on moonshiners.

If you are building fixtures for your livestock you will also have to get permits on these based on their sizes. Also, if you live in a residential area you will have to make sure you are allowed certain animals. Chickens and rabbits should not be a problem but localities may not allow you to raise goats and sheep outside in a neighborhood.

Next comes from bartering and the tax man. Make sure you are not producing too much for trade, the point here is to become self-sufficient after a while anyways so as you go this problem should correct itself. If you begin trading and selling too much, you may be required by law to pay taxes on it.

As I mentioned before, you must be aware of this so your new lifestyle is not halted or inconvenienced by local authorities. It would be horrible if you invest a lot of time and money into making this lifestyle change if the local government comes and shuts you down. Go to your local government to find out if you are able to do everything and what permits you may need. Get everything documented and organized because there may be people not used to your self-sufficient means so if anyone complains, you've got proof you are in the right. There shouldn't be any problems here but it is best to be prepared.

Putting It All Together

At this point, you've got all the information you need to change to a completely self-sufficient, "Off the Grid" lifestyle. We've covered a comprehensive list of subjects including utility alternatives and personal crops and livestock but that is only the start because that is what you need to live.

You can further explore cooking. Who is to say you can't go on to enjoy carpentry? What about learning to craft your own beer or wine? Life off the grid doesn't have to be void of luxury. Just as the growing process relates to learning how to raise livestock, it also relates to growing through life motivators. Survival is just the beginning.

Of course, more research is required to do everything more effectively but in the end your experiences will be the best teacher for you. Simply put though, your meals will never have tasted so good. You will begin to truly consider the effort behind electricity and running water. Your life will never have been so free from outside constraints.

Say goodbye to utility and grocery bills. Say goodbye to depending on others. Say goodbye to the frustrations and pressures of a connected life.

And, since I hate books that end on a negative note: Say hello to self-dependence. Say hello to meaningful work. Say hello to true freedom and self-appreciation.

From The Author

Thank you for taking the time to read this book. As an author, I understand the importance of creating books which my readers will find both enjoyable and informative. If you have the time and feel generous, please don't hesitate to leave an honest review of this book.......... Henry Hill

Other Books By Henry Hill

Survival Pantry

Do know what you'll eat in the event of a disaster?

Survival Pantry presents the essential elements that you should consider in preparing yourself and your family for the eventuality of an unforeseen disaster. There are certain things that are necessary for humans to survive.

First, we need an adequate supply of clean water. This book will enable you determine the amount of water you will need to provide for you and your family. The quantity of water you need will depend on how severe the disaster is and how long it takes to get things back to normal. It will also depend on what sources of water that are accessible to you.

Secondly, we need an adequate supply of non-perishable food adapted to the individual needs of your family members. This book will walk you through how to compile your emergency readiness supplies and what to consider first for the short term. In addition, it will show you how you can build on the short term for a longer term supply. You will learn methods of preserving food so that it is still edible and nutritious in the future when you need it.

A major crisis always takes us by surprise, but we do not have to be unprepared. This book will provide you with peace of mind now, knowing that should something happen in the future, you have done what you can to ensure the well-being and safety of the people you love.

The Prepper's Guide To Economic Collapse Survival

"Paper is poverty,... it is only the ghost of money, and not money itself".........Thomas Jefferson 1788

There are plenty of signs that indicate our world is headed towards financial collapse. We have become dependent on paper money that is quickly losing value. What will you do when paper money is completely worthless? Will you be able to feed the family or provide shelter? How will you manage basic problems like finding clean drinking water and obtaining the things you need? These are all problems that you will be confronted with in the aftermath of the stock market crashing or a war that kills the economy.

This book will take you by the hand and lead you down the road to prepping for a major economic collapse. You will have to learn a lot of new skills. When grocery store shelves are empty and the malls are closed, you have to find food and make your own clothes. When money isn't good for anything more than starting a fire, you will have to learn how to operate on a barter system. To use the bartering system, you need to know what to store today that will have high value in a world where paper money is useless. Don't get caught empty handed when the economy tanks. Get started with your prepping today.

www.ingramcontent.com/pod-product-compliance
Lightning Source LLC
Chambersburg PA
CBHW060444290526
45793CB00002B/569